D0621007

What in the World Is a Piano?

Mary Elizabeth Salzmann

Consulting Editor, Diane Craig, M.A./Reading Specialist

A Division of ABDO

ABDO
Publishing Company

visit us at www.abdopublishing.com

Printed in the United States of America, North Mankato, Minnesota
092011
012012

 PRINTED ON RECYCLED PAPER

Editor: Elissa Mann
Content Developer: Nancy Tuminelly
Cover and Interior Design: Colleen Dolphin, Mighty Media, Inc.
Interior Production: Kelsey Gullickson
Photo Credits: Shutterstock, Thinkstock

Library of Congress Cataloging-in-Publication Data

Salzmann, Mary Elizabeth, 1968-

What in the world is a piano? / Mary Elizabeth Salzmann.

p. cm. -- (Musical instruments)

ISBN 978-1-61783-207-9

1. Piano--Juvenile literature. I. Title.

ML650.S16 2012

786.2'19--dc23

                      2011023172

Super SandCastle™ books are created by a team of professional educators, reading specialists, and content developers around five essential components—phonemic awareness, phonics, vocabulary, text comprehension, and fluency—to assist young readers as they develop reading skills and strategies and increase their general knowledge. All books are written, reviewed, and leveled for guided reading, early reading intervention, and Accelerated Reader® programs for use in shared, guided, and independent reading and writing activities to support a balanced approach to literacy instruction.

Contents

What Is a

A piano is a musical instrument.

piano?

The **main** parts of a piano are the soundboard, strings, hammers, keyboard, keys, music rest, and **pedals**. Most pianos have 88 keys. There are 52 white keys and 36 black keys.

soundboard

keyboard

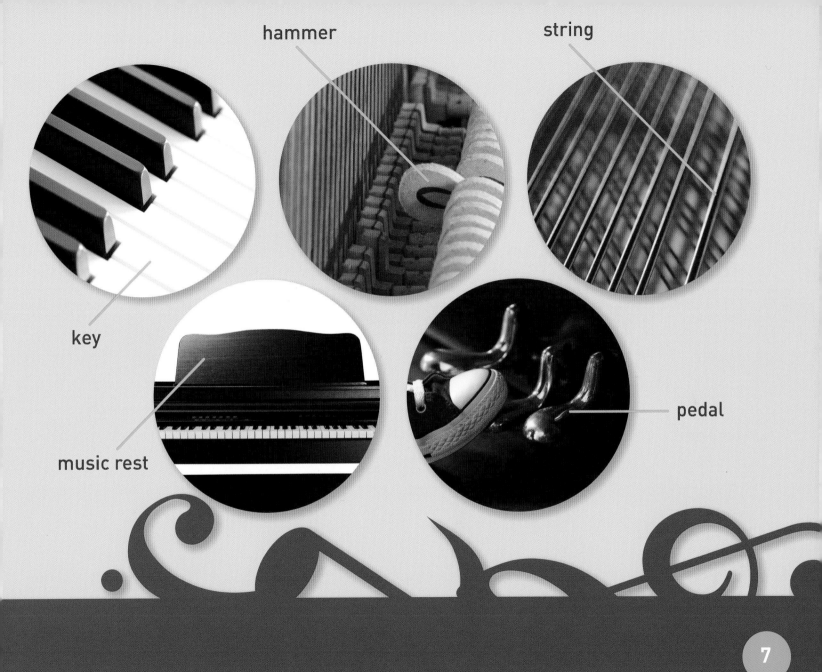

hammer

string

key

music rest

pedal

There are grand pianos and upright pianos. In a grand piano, the soundboard and strings lie flat.

In an upright piano, the soundboard and strings are vertical.

To play the piano, the piano player presses the piano keys. Pressing a key makes a hammer strike a string to play a note. Each key plays a different note.

There are also **electric** and digital pianos. Sometimes they are called electronic keyboards.

Electric pianos can have strings but many do not. Often electric pianos can sound like other instruments.

Let's Play

the Piano!

Madeline is playing a grand piano. She has been taking piano **lessons** for three years.

Richard and his dad are practicing a new song on the piano. Richard wants to play it for his mom on her birthday.

Lily has a piano **lesson** every Monday. Between lessons, she practices for an hour each day.

Jesse is playing an **electric** keyboard. He likes all the different ways it can sound.

Find the Piano

d. guitar   **c.** clarinet   **b.** piano (correct)   **a.** flute

Piano Quiz

1. Piano keys are blue and red. True or False?

2. There is only one kind of piano. True or False?

3. Each piano key plays a different note. True or False?

4. All **electric** pianos have strings. True or False?

5. Madeline plays a grand piano. True or False?

ANSWERS: 1. false 2. false 3. true 4. false 5. true

Glossary

electric – needing to be plugged into an outlet in order to work.

lesson – a period of time when a skill or topic is studied or taught.

main – the most important or the biggest.

pedal – the part of a piano or bicycle that is moved by the foot.